William Sturch

Apeleutherus

Or an Effort to Attain Intellectual Freedom

William Sturch

Apeleutherus
Or an Effort to Attain Intellectual Freedom

ISBN/EAN: 9783337022488

Printed in Europe, USA, Canada, Australia, Japan

Cover: Foto ©Lupo / pixelio.de

More available books at **www.hansebooks.com**

APELEUTHERUS;

OR,

AN EFFORT TO ATTAIN

INTELLECTUAL FREEDOM.

IN THREE PARTS.

I. ON PUBLIC WORSHIP.

II. ON RELIGIOUS INSTRUCTION.

III. ON CHRISTIANITY AS A SUPERNATURAL
COMMUNICATION.

—— neque noſtræ diſputationes quicquam aliud agunt, niſi ut, in utramque partem dicendo, eliciant, et tanquam exprimant aliquid, quod aut verum ſit, aut ad id, quam proxume accedat. CIC. ACADEM. Lib. ii.

When I was a child, I ſpake as a child, I underſtood as a child, I thought as a child; but when I became a man, I put away childiſh things. PAUL, I Cor. xiii.

In regard to religious matters, there is an intellectual cowardice jnſtilled into the mind of the people from their infancy, which prevents their enquiry. Credulity is made an indiſpenſable virtue ; to enquire, or exert their reaſon, is denounced as ſinful ; and in the catholic church is puniſhed with more ſeveie penances than moral crimes. DARWIN's Zoonomia, Vol. ii.

LONDON:

PRINTED FOR J. JOHNSON, IN ST. PAUL'S CHURCH-YARD,
By Thomas Benſley, Bolt-Court, Fleet-Street.

1799.
[Price Two SHILLINGS in Boards.]

DEDICATION.

D. O. M.

O Thou, whofe bounty gave this mantling bower
 Where, from the world retired, I oft recline,
 And trace thy wonder-working hand divine,
And read thy name in every blufhing flower;
Sovereign of nature, all-directing power!
 Great fource of being, life, and light, and joy!
 To Thee I dedicate this beft employ,
This fweeteft folace of the filent hour.
O fearch this heart, that feeks no vain difguife,
 Accept the tribute, and the labour blefs:
View the pure motive with approving eyes—
 Thy glory, in thy creatures happinefs.
Smile on the page that bids the mind be free,
And points the path to Virtue, and to Thee!

PREFACE.

The desire of knowledge, if it be cherish-
ed with a view to the improvement of moral
practice, and the increase of human feli-
city, is, of all the qualities and dispositions of
the mind, the most honourable to its posses-
sor. But if he would derive from it all the
advantage of which it is capable, or accom-
plish in any important degree his noble aim,
it must be cultivated with unbounded freedom, and with ardent affection. No doctrine
must in his estimation be so unquestionable,
no authority so sacred, as to bar enquiry. He
must be, in the best and most extensive sense
of the phrase, a FREETHINKER. Nor must
the lover of truth be diverted from his object
by the difficulties which he will have to en-
counter in the pursuit of it. The acquisition
of so precious a jewel will be to him a full

recom-

recompence for all his labour : and being once
in poffeffion of it, though he may not, perhaps, think it prudent at all times to expofe
it to the view of others, left he fhould be caft-
ing his pearl before fwine, he will himfelf
value it above all earthly treafure, and will
never be induced, by any confideration, to
abandon it.

The liberal enquirer, indeed, cannot be expected to feel that attachment to fyftem, and
that degree of zeal for the converfion of
others, which is known to animate thofe who
profefs what is commonly called orthodoxy;
and who fuppofing the favour of Heaven to be
confined to the belief of a fet of fpeculative
notions, fome of which they acknowledge to
be unintelligible, muft confequently, if they
have the common feelings of humanity, be
anxioufly concerned for their general reception. He who is perfuaded, that it is the
uniform and unchangeable doctrine, both of
natural and fupernatural religion, that *every
upright man muft be happy* in every ftage of his
exiftence,

exiftence, is no farther defirous of the prevalence of any opinion, than as it appears to
be calculated to affect moral practice. He
has often had occafion to obferve—fuch is the
bias in favour of virtue in the human conftitution—that to FEAR GOD AND TO DEPART
FROM EVIL, are difpofitions by no means
peculiar to any fpeculative fyftem: and if he
find a man in poffeffion of thefe genuine evidences of TRUE WISDOM, he cannot perfuade
himfelf to indulge any very deep diftrefs about
the abfurdity of his faith. The reputed or-
thodox therefore may hold faft and inculcate
their dogmas, without abridging his happinefs; and if what he may offer on his part
be received with candour and attention, his
wifhes are completely gratified.

The author is perfectly aware, that this is
too much to hope for the following effays
from the generality of readers; and it is this
confideration that has determined him,
though reluctantly, to fend his little book
into the world *without his name.* He feels

no

no inward reproach on reviewing this employment of his leifure hours. He appre-
hends no cenfure, from the truly liberal and
enlightened, on its publication. But while he
fees no important purpofe to be anfwered, by
the difclofure of his name; he thinks himfelf
juftified, in yielding to confiderations of pru-
dence and perfonal quiet. He views with
admiration, that intrepidity of foul, and firm-
nefs of nerve, which enable a man to encoun-
ter the fcorn of fuperftition, and the rage of
bigotry. He honours the bold fpirit of a
Luther, and a Wakefield; the fearlefs integrity of a Price, and a Prieftley : but he con-
feffes that he is unequal to the imitation of
thefe illuftrious characters—he renounces all
claim to any portion of the praife, which is
fo juftly their due—he is unambitious of re-
putation—he courts obfcurity.

It has long been his favourite maxim, that
it behoves every man to devote fome portion
of his life to the public; to aim at fomething
by which his fellow men may be advantaged.

Every

Every man, indeed, does not poffefs the powers of a Locke or a Hartley; but the means and opportunities of advancing the public weal are infinitely various; and fingularly hard muft be the lot of him who can truly fay, that he is, by nature or by fortune, utterly incapable, in any degree or in any manner, of deferving well of his country and of mankind. *In magna copia rerum, aliud alii natura iter often-dit* *. And if in thefe humble effays, the author fhall have been able to contribute any thing towards the demolition of the old and tottering fabric of error and fuperftition; if he fhall have added only a few " grains of gun-powder†," to that train which is deftined,

* Salluft. Bell. Catalin.

† " The prefent filent propagation of truth may even " be compared to thofe caufes in nature which lie dormant " for a time, but which in proper circumftances act with " the greateft effect. We are, as it were, laying gun- " powder, grain by grain, under the old building of error " and fuperftition, &c." PRIESTLEY on the Importance and Extent of Free Inquiry, p. 40.

The alarm occafioned by the ufe of this harmlefs metaphorical language was highly ridiculous. I fhall not eafily forget

tined, fooner or later, to level it with the
ground; he will have reafon to thank Heaven,
that he has not lived in vain.

He is willing to flatter himfelf, that if his
views of the feveral fubjects of which he has
treated be juft, the communication of his
thoughts may be of ufe to others. If, on the
contrary, the voice of impartial and judicious
criticifm fhould pronounce them to be falfe
and groundlefs, he earneftly hopes they will
make no impreffion. If he has failed, however, it has not been through hafte or inattention. He does not prefent to his readers
what coft him nothing; but the refult of
long-continued and ferious meditation. It

forget being in the gallery of the Houfe of Commons, when
the refpectable member for Oxford, Sir W, D. with a tone
of voice and a countenance,

" That witneffed huge affliction and difmay,"

announced the difcovery of this new gunpowder plot! The
confternation of the worthy Baronet could fcarcely have
been greater, if he had actually found a fecond Guy Faux
with his matches and dark lantern, ready to explode his
thirty-fix barrels of real gunpowder, to the- deftruction of
King, Lords, and Commons!

8   would

would have been comparatively eafy to have written volumes; but as truth gains nothing by prolix differtation, he has been at confiderable pains to comprefs his ideas into the compafs of three fhort effays; and he trufts he has done it fo as to avoid obfcurity. If the reafoning in the two firft of thefe effays be correct, it will appear, that the clerical profeffion is one of thofe which, without lofs to the world, might be wholly difcontinued. And if, in the third, he has fucceeded in endeavouring to exhibit a faithful fketch of genuine chriftianity, it will follow, that in whatever eftimation it may defervedly be held, as a luminous and comprehenfive fcheme of religion and morals, it is neither poffible, nor of much importance, to determine with certainty, whether its pretenfions to fupernatural authority be true or falfe.

He has only to add, that his motives are of the pureft kind. No party connexion or private intereft, has corrupted his mind, or warped his judgment. He can difcern no merit,

merit, either in a bigoted attachment to received opinions on the one hand, or in a rage for departing from them as widely as poſſible, on the other. It is the firſt wiſh of his heart, that the light of TRUTH may be more and more extenſively diffuſed, and that in proportion to its diffuſion, the human race may become virtuous and happy.

September 1, 1799.

APELEUTHERUS.

PART I.

ON PUBLIC WORSHIP.

THE being, the perfections, and the providence, of the Supreme Eternal Spirit whom we
call GOD, are clearly manifeſt in the conſtitu-
tion and courſe of nature. The perception and
belief of theſe ſublime truths indeed, and conſequently their influence on the conduct, will be,
as in all other caſes, ſtronger or weaker, in proportion to the attention that is paid to them. To
the obſerving mind they muſt neceſſarily be the
ſubject of frequent meditation and reflection;
and ſometimes, eſpecially in ſeaſons of difficulty,
they will be recollected by the moſt careleſs and
diſſipated of mankind. In the former will be
produced habitual reverence, gratitude, love, and

confidence;

confidence; and thefe affections, whether ex-
preffed in words or not, will naturally rife from
the feeling heart, like pure incenfe from the altar,
towards that Being who " is good to all, and
whofe tender mercies are over all his works*."
And even the latter, whofe general character is fuppofed to be inattention and thoughtleffnefs, though
he may be little difpofed to " praife the Lord for his
goodnefs†," will not be able, in the hour of cala-
mity, when all human help feems to fail, to avoid
wifhing, and even *praying*, for that protection
and affiftance which can only be afforded by HIM
who " ruleth by his power for ever ‡." In fhort,
prayer naturally follows the belief of a God: and
to fuppofe a finite dependent creature, living under a fenfe of divine providence, and impreffed
with thofe feelings which are the genuine fruit of
juft views of his glorious character, and yet ab-
ftaining wholly from *any fort* of direct addrefs to
him, feems contrary to all experience, and abfurd in itfelf.

* Pf. cxlv. 9. † Pf. cvii. ‡ Pf. lxvi. 7.

But,

has never pictured any benefits to be derived from public worſhip, which can compenſate for the direful conſequences of ſectarian zeal. The former may perhaps have contributed ſomething to the conſolation of pious ignorance; the latter has deluged the world with blood!

Again. It has been ſaid, that it is our duty to endeavour to impreſs the minds of thoſe with whom we are connected, and eſpecially of the members of our own family, with religious and moral ideas; and that public worſhip is a means to this end. The reply is, that this end, important beyond all that language can expreſs, may be more effectually anſwered, by private inſtruction and exhortation, both regular and occaſional; by recommending to them ſuch books as are beſt calculated to inform their underſtandings, and to inſpire them with the love of truth and goodneſs; and, above all, by ſetting before them, in our own perſons, an uniform and conſiſtent example of integrity and virtue. It is, however, by no means the intention of the writer to affirm, that when a private family, or a ſmall number of friends, are

aſſembled

affembled for any important purpofe—for inftance,
when they fit down together for mutual inftruction and improvement, by reading or converfation—they are not at liberty, if they find themfelves fo difpofed, to unite in fome fhort acknowledgment of their common dependence upon one
fupreme Being, and fome concife petition for his
bleffing and protection.   But, againft all difcur-
five, didactic, doctrinal, defcriptive, and narrative
prayer, and generally againft all long detailed
addreffes to the Deity, *upon any occafion whatever,* he ftrenuoufly protefts, as abfurd and unreafonable, and fubverfive of the very end which
they profefs to have in view; by creating in the
minds of young perfons a difguft and averfion
from religion and every thing connected with it,
which frequently remains, fixed and infuperable,
to the lateft period of life.

Still farther, it is faid, that whatever may be
thought of public prayer and pfalm-finging, it
cannot be doubted that *preaching* is of the utmoft
importance, as a means of inftructing mankind in
their duty, and teaching them " how they ought

to

to walk and to pleafe God;" and therefore, though we may not be able to perceive any great advantage arifing from public worfhip, feparately confidered; yet, as it is ufually accompanied by difcourfes calculated to imprefs the mind with a fenfe of the great importance of religious and moral practice, it is in this view entitled to our warmeft encouragement. To this it may be replied, that admitting for the prefent the utility of preaching, till we come to treat exprefsly on it in the next effay—this argument will have no force, unlefs it can be fhewn, that public worfhip and preaching are neceffarily connected. But this is by no means the cafe. Nothing is fo eafy as to feparate them. And if it be acknowledged that the former is abfurd, while the latter is fuppofed to be ufeful, furely the obvious courfe is, to abolifh the one, and to retain the other.

But " is not a regular and conflant attendance on public worfhip, a very proper method of improving the leifure of the Sabbath ; which might be dangerous if not ftatedly occupied in

C   fome

fome mode or other, and cannot be fo well em-
ployed in any other way?" The Sabbath! By
what authority do we prohibit the innocent and
ufeful occupations of life on any particular day*?
By what right do we enjoin idlenefs, the parent
of vice, during a feventh portion of time? By
whofe command do we keep, or rather pretend
to keep, the Sabbath?

" By his, who forbade the eating of fwine,
who inftituted the paffover, and appointed cir-
cumcifion."

Why then do we not abftain from pork, keep
the paffover, and circumcife our children?

" Becaufe we are not Jews."

. For the fame reafon we have no concern with
the Sabbath. Are we ftill to learn that we have

* See this fubject fully difcuffed in Evanfon's " Arguments
againft and for the fabbatical obfervance of Sunday." See alfo
Belfham's Review of Wilberforce, Letter 12; a work in which
perfect good temper, clofenefs of reafoning, perfpicuity of
arrangement, and purity of ftyle, unite to form one of the
moft mafterly controverfial books of the age; and to place the
character of the excellent author, as a gentleman, a philofopher, and a chriftian, above any praife which I am able to
beftow.

nothing

nothing to do with Jewiſh inſtitutions—that they are peculiar to that people—that they were in-, tended by their legiſlator as a mark or ſign of ſeparation between them and the reſt of the world—that Moſes and the prophets, though full of denunciations againſt the people of Iſrael, on account of their diſregard of the Sabbath, never once ſpeak of that inſtitution as univerſally obli- gatory; never once exhort the Gentiles to the obſervance of it; never once threaten them with puniſhment for the negleĉt of it—that in faĉt it is a merely national inſtitution—and that we who are not Jews, are no more intereſted in it, than in their diſtinĉtion of meats and drinks, or their new moons—and that conſequently, the horror with which many pious perſons contem- plate the idea of *profaning the ſabbath*, is a mere child of the imagination, utterly deſtitute of foundation in truth or reaſon? With us all days are equal: and were the affairs of the world conduĉted according to the diĉtates of reaſon, and the benevolent maxims of chriſtianity, no day would by any claſs of mankind be ſo entirely de-

voted

voted to labour, as not to afford leifure for felf-recollection, and for intellectual and moral improvement *.

By this time, perhaps, fome frequenter of public worfhip is ready to admit, that little good is likely to arife from it. Still, however, the influence of early prejudice prevails; and he is unwilling to difcontinue a practice to which he has been fo long accuftomed. His mind is ftill haunted by a notion, that it is a *duty*. But how does this appear? Not from nature, which is totally filent upon the fubject. Not from the New Teftament, which has nothing in favour of it. If it be a duty at all, it muft be capable of being defined. But no individual can difcover, either from natural or fupernatural revelation,

* Such is the force of prejudice, that the crime of Sabbath-breaking, in the eftimation of fome people, equals the greateft moral guilt! It is not long fince, that I heard a very worthy divine, in a difcourfe on the exceeding finfulnefs of fin, ufe nearly the following words: " Depend upon it, my bre-" thren, no murderer, no adulterer, no perjured perfon, no " liar, no thief, no *Sabbath breaker*, fhall have any portion in " the kingdom of God and of Chrift through all eternity!" When he had proceeded thus far, he might with equal juf-tice have added, no taylor, no fhoemaker, &c.

the

the place where, the manner how, or the perfons in conjunction with whom, it is his duty to
perform this act. Nor can it indeed be performed at all, by any reafonable man, except under
very peculiar circumftances. Such a man will
not believe that he is called upon by any law,
natural or fupernatural, to do what appears to
him to be either irrational or immoral. He cannot, therefore, concur in any mode of worfhip
which he conceives to be abfurd, or of evil tendency. He muft wait till he is fo fortunate as
to find a number of perfons like-minded with
himfelf, who are agreed, or ready to agree, in
fome fcheme of public worfhip which he fhall
think rational and ufeful. Now, whether this is
ever likely to happen to *any* man who *thinks for
himfelf*, inftead of refigning his underftanding to
the authority of cuftom and fafhion, let the
reader judge.

Laftly. It has been contended, that the idea
of public prayer being unreafonable in itfelf,
and difcountenanced by Jefus Chrift, is utterly

irrecon-

irreconcileable with the fact, of its being fo generally practifed by his followers.   But this argu-
gument will " vanifh into thin air," if we confider, by whom, and for what reafons, the practice has been promoted and encouraged.   The
performance of what is called *divine fervice*, and
the adminiftration of *facraments*, require a body
of men, fet apart for that purpofe; and if they
can perfuade the people, as they have been too
fuccefsful in attempting, that thefe things are of
the utmoft importance, and that they are only
valid when under their management, and depend
for all their efficacy upon paffing through their
facred hands; they immediately obtain an af-
cendency over their minds, and a command of
their wealth, which are too valuable to be eafily
relinquifhed; and which, when acquired, they
will naturally be difpofed to employ every art
and every argument, to extend and to perpetuate.

On the whole, it appears,—That public, ftated
worfhip is not reafonable, becaufe it is not the
worfhip of the heart, nor is capable of expreff-
ing the various affections and feelings of the feveral

veral individuals who compofe a numerous affembly; it gives occafion to hypocrify and to
falfe notions; it is difcountenanced by the New
Teftament; its tendency is to difguife, obfcure,
and corrupt, the purity, fimplicity, and fpiritu-
ality of real religion, as dictated by nature and
confirmed by Jefus Chrift: and though, as happens in other cafes, its actual effect is not generally fo bad as might be expected, yet it muft be
allowed to be confiderable—That fhort occafional
addreffes to the Deity, may fometimes be offered
jointly by a few perfons, not only without abfurdity, but with advantage. But, that the worfhip " in fpirit and in truth" in the beft fenfe of
the words, that which is of univerfal concern,
and of the higheft importance, is that SECRET
COMMUNION, which the truly pious mind never
fails to hold with its Creator; which is perfectly natural, and even unavoidable; which is
agreeable to reafon, is productive of the hap-
pieft moral and religious effects, and is fanc-
tioned by the authority of our Lord Jefus Chrift,
both in precept and example. The true wor-

fhipper,

fhipper is not he " who is one outwardly ;" not
he who offers his ftated, formal, and ceremonious
homage, at Jerufalem or on mount Gerizim, in
the temple, or in the conventicle: but he is the
true worfhipper " who is one inwardly;" and
acceptable worfhip is of the heart, and not of
the tongue, whofe praife is not of man, but of
GOD.

PART

PART II.

ON RELIGIOUS INSTRUCTION.

THAT religious and moral inftruction is of the very firft importance to the young, and that thofe who are more advanced in years are ftill capable of deriving great advantages from frequent attention to thefe fubjects, are truths which will be readily affented to by every man who himfelf values religion and morals, and who has made any confiderable progrefs in the ftudy of human nature. It appears to be the immutable law of Divine Providence, that nothing valuable is to be obtained without labour. And as in the vegetable kingdom, whatever may be the fecundity of the earth, no good fruit is to be expected but in confequence of the unremitting care, and affiduous exertions of the hufbandman; fo in the moral world, whatever we may imagine con-

6   cerning

cerning the original powers and difpofitions of human nature, we cannot rationally hope for excellence of chara&er, but in proportion as due pains have been beftowed upon the cultivation of the mind. If then it be our duty to promote the welfare of human fociety, and efpecially to fe-cure the happinefs of thofe individuals who are placed under our more immediate prote&ion, we are furely called upon by the moft urgent mo-tives, to ufe every method in our power to " train them up in the way in which they fhould walk," in the reafonable hope that " when they are old they will not depart from it*."

There is then no queftion concerning the pro-priety or neceffity of education. But the expe-diency of an enquiry concerning the *beft and moft effectual means* of inftruction, is fo obvious, that it has exercifed the underftandings and the pens of philofophers in all ages. The fubje& how-ever is not yet exhaufted; and I now propofe to fubmit a few fhort obfervations upon it, to the judgment of the reader.

* Prov. xxii. 6.

Againft

Againſt very early inſtruction it has been ob-
jected, that its effect is to ſtore the mind with pre-
judices inſtead of uſeful knowledge; and to pre-
clude the poſſibility of forming an impartial
judgment at a riper age. But in anſwer to this
objection it may be ſaid, that if admitted, it
would conclude againſt all inſtruction whatever;
and would leave every individual of the human
race, to trace his ſolitary path through life, un-
aſſiſted by the reſearches and experience of the
reſt of his ſpecies. All inſtruction whatever
may be conſidered as operating in the way of
prejudice. Every mechanic or liberal art which
contributes to the comfort and convenience of
life; every diſcovery by which ſcience ameliorates
the condition of humanity; every thing in the
long and ſlow gradation, from untutored nature,
to the moſt improved civilization ; in a word,
every thing that diſtinguiſhes the philoſopher
from the ſavage, is, and muſt be, received and
acted upon by the generality of mankind, without the poſſibility of any previous enquiry concerning the reaſons upon which it is founded.
Theſe

Thefe reafons indeed are open to fubfequent inveftigation, and *ought by all means to be examined.*
But in the firft inftance, to act from habit, formed by precept and example, and not from the
deductions of reafon, is the univerfal and unchangeable condition of humanity; and were a
practice fo abfurd as that of deferring moral and
religious inftruction till the maturity of the pupil, to prevail, fad experience would fhew, that
it would then come too late.   The enemy being
already in poffeffion of the field, it would be over-
fpread with tares of idlenefs and vice, which no
human fkill would be able to eradicate *.

                                      Difmiffing

* This effay was written before the appearance of Mifs
Hannah More's Strictures on Female Education, in the beginning of whofe tenth chapter there is a coincidence of ideas,
and (allowing for the fuperior talents of the fair author) a
fimilarity of language fomewhat remarkable.   I wifh I could
fpeak with approbation of *every* part of a work in which there
is fo much that is truly valuable; but, alas! it is unhappily
disfigured by an exploded and abfurd fyftem of divinity, as
irreconcileable to unprejudiced reafon, as to the New Teftament.   Mifs M. confiders it as a "foundation truth" that
children are not innocent beings, but "bring into the world
a corrupt nature and evil difpofitions;" and "the quality moft
important in an inftructor of youth," fhe fays, is "a ftrong
                                      impreffion

Difmiffing then this extravagant objection as unworthy of an enlightened philofophy, we proceed to obferve, that as the only method of fe-

impreffion of the corruption of our nature." The pupil, no doubt, is to be taught this " foundation truth." If fo, what an excufe will it not furnifh him for all irregularities of conduct! what a ready anfwer to every reproof of his tutor! " You tell me that I am naturally wicked. I follow my inclinations. How can you blame me for acting agreeably to nature ?"—How oppofite is all this 'to genuine Chriftianity! In the New Teftament, young children are every where reprefented as free from evil difpofitions, innocent, and teachable. The corrupt nature fo much infifted upon, was the invention of priefts in an after age, in order to magnify the importance of baptifm, and confequently to increafe the power and authority of the clergy. But what fays our divine mafter, whofe kingdom was not of this world? Except ye be converted *and become as little children,* ye fhall not enter into the kingdom of heaven, Matt. xviii. 3. Suffer *little children* to come unto me, for *of fuch* is the kingdom of heaven, Matt. xix. 13. Mark x. 14. Whofoever fhall not receive the kingdom of God as a *little child* fhall in no wife enter therein, Luke xviii. 17. What fays an Apoftle? In malice be ye *children,* 1 Cor. xiv. 20. In perfect confiftency with this groundlefs notion, our ingenious and well intentioned author feems to have adopted the ridiculous fancy of an ancient father, who contended, that the beft works of thofe who were not Chriftians were no more than *fplendida peccata,* or, in the language of the thirteenth article of the Church of England, that good works " have the nature of fin." Yet with ftrange inconfiftency, fhe has recourfe to the hiftories of Greece and Rome for inftances of pure morals and illuftrious virtue!

curing

curing the opening mind from thofe falfe im-
preffions which it will be liable to receive from
the corrupt maxims and vicious practice of the
world, is to pre-occupy it with juft views and
virtuous habits; we need not hefitate to adopt
the decifion of the wifeft and moft enlightened of
mankind, who have concurred in affuring us,
that a courfe of moral difcipline ought to be en-
tered, upon as foon as the capacity of the fubject fhall render it poffible. That this ability to
receive inftruction difcovers itfelf very early, is
well known to thofe who are converfant with
children; and it is certain that a boy of four or
five years of age may be made to underftand the
meaning, and to feel the importance, of the
leading truths in morals and religion, in a degree
that would be abfolutely incredible without experi-
ment. During the years of childhood we acquire
thofe ideas and habits which are to influence the
whole of our exiftence; and on the improvement or neglect of this early period of life, this pre-
c ious feed time of the mind, depends, for the moft
part, the happinefs or mifery of the future man.

By

By whom then is this falutary inftruction to be afforded to the infant mind? Nature, faithful Nature, inftantly dictates the reply. By thofe to whom the great author of our being, the all-wife contriver and governor of the eternal fyftem, has immediately intrufted it. By PARENTS, the natural guardians of the lives, the health, the fortunes, and the morals of the rifing generation.

That the bufinefs of moral difcipline properly belongs to parents, is evident from hence, that they only can be fuppofed to feel that intereft in the improvement of their pupils, which is effential to complete fuccefs in this important work. The neareft and moft neceffary connexion between individuals of the human race is that of families; confifting of the relation of hufband and wife, parent and child. Thefe little focieties are the fources of whatever is delightful and confoling to human nature; and on the good government of thefe depends, under Providence, the prefervation of order, morality, religion, in a word, of

all

all that is valuable to mankind *. Other teachers, indeed, may from a fenfe of duty be ftimulated to exertions at once honourable to themfelves and beneficial to thofe under their care; but this principle is, in general, too cold to produce thofe vigorous and perfevering efforts which are the natural fruit of parental affection. Other teachers are liable to be difheartened by dulnefs, or difgufted by obftinacy: but the zeal of the parent

---

* If however we give credit to the advocates for the perpetuation of ignorance and flavery, it is from the civil and ecclefiaftical powers, that have kindly undertaken to manage the affairs of nations, that we derive all our bleffings. Kings and priefts, they affure us, are not only wife and good themfelves, but moreover the caufe of all that is wife and good in others; and from the abolition of thefe orders, which many think feems to be faft approaching, they predict the moft fatal confequences. This doctrine, however, labours under the misfortune of being contradicted by univerfal hiftory. Kings and priefts have in all ages been the great difturbers of the world; and to their luft of dominion is to be afcribed the far greater part of the evils which have afflicted mankind. When I fpeak of *families*, therefore, as fources of happinefs, I by no means intend *Royal* families; and if I mention FATHERS, as the proper guides and inftructors of youth, I muft not be underftood to include *Right Rev.* FATHERS *in God.* Not a word of this note however applies to our own moft gracious fovereign, or to his illuftrious houfe, of whom, both from my own inclination, as well as *in obedience to Act of Parliament,* I always wifh to fpeak and to think with refpect.

never

never cools; his hope never dies. He ftill flatters himfelf that his labours will be finally fuccefsful. And as " the hufbandman waiteth for the precious fruit of the earth, and hath long patience for it *," fo the fond parent, under circumftances of difficulty and difcouragement, which would drive to defpair any lefs interefted teacher, is fupported by the cheering hope, that he fhall one day enjoy the reward of his labours, in the wifdom and virtue of his fon.

Nor is it natural affection alone, that renders parents the proper guardians and inftructors of their offspring. The fenfe of duty, which we juft now mentioned, is more powerful in them than it can be fuppofed to be in any other clafs of mankind.

The father of a family is invefted with a truft, the importance of which he cannot eftimate too highly; and is under an obligation, from which nothing can releafe him, to devote all his powers, corporeal and mental, principally to one great object; namely, to the gradual advancement in wif-

* James v. 7.

D   dom

dom and virtue, and confequently in happinefs, of thofe beings whom, by the appointment of Heaven, he has been inftrumental in introducing into the world. It is his indifpenfable duty, not only to provide them, or to enable them to provide themfelves, with things needful for the body; but, which is of infinitely greater importance, to furnifh their minds with fuch principles, as may enable them to fupport an upright and confiftent conduct, and to bear an ufeful and honourable part in the tranfactions of this unftable fcene. I fay, *to act well here.* I know that much has been faid about preparation for eternity; and in this view, great ftrefs has been laid, *for a very obvious reafon,* already noticed, on the efficacy of facraments and ceremonial obfervances. But if, agreeably to the general expectation of mankind in all ages, there be an *hereafter,* no unprejudiced man can doubt, that whatever dignifies and ennobles human nature, and renders it in a great meafure fuperior to the chances and changes of mortality, muft be the only poffible preparation

for

for the untried and unknown employments of the future and invifible world.

This imperious duty, the reflecting father can- not but ftrongly feel. " Heaven," he will fay, looking upon his helplefs infant, " has committed to my charge this tender plant, to be reared to maturity; and if through my fupinenefs it wither and die, or living, produce not its proper fruit, how fhall I render up my account! If, through my criminal negligence, this rational and moral being fail to attain that which is the perfection of its nature, and the end of its creation, WISDOM, VIRTUE, and HAPPINESS, furely Heaven will re- quire it at my hands! Neceffity is laid upon me; Woe is unto me, if I fhrink from this important tafk. I fee my duty, and I will per- form it. My whole foul fhall engage in the work; and though it is not in me to command fuccefs, I am determined to deferve it*."

From thefe confiderations, if we miftake not,

* 'Tis not in mortals to command fuccefs,
But we'll do more, Sempronius—we'll deferve it.
ADDISON's CATO.

the

the enquiring mind will be irrefiftibly led to con-
demn the monftrous abfurdity of that fyftem,
which would diveft parents of the exercife of their
natural right to educate their offspring, and tranf-
fer it to the ftate; agreeably to the practice of
the celebrated Spartans, and fome other nations.
In Sparta indeed, where public glory, and not
private happinefs, was the object of the government, where the ftate feemed not to be made for
men, but men for the ftate, this practice might
be very confiftent. It was neceffary that individuals fhould be formed and trained to the views
and ends of the body politic. But if there be a
nation upon earth in which liberty and equality
are firft principles; in which the welfare of all
the members of the fociety, without preference
and without exception, is the great end of the
inftitution—in fuch a nation one might hope,
that inftead of *legal* truth and *national* inftruction, every man would be fecured in that perfect
and unbounded liberty of educating his offspring,
which is not only his original and natural right,
but without which there can be no rational hope

of

of any confiderable and fubftantial improvement
in human affairs.

It is true that hitherto almoft all governments
have, more or lefs, interfered with the facred
right of education. But what does this prove,
except that hitherto, there has exifted no fuch
thing as a perfectly rational government in the
world? If this be doubted, and if any ftill feel
inclined to adopt the unnatural opinion, that the
bufinefs of religious education is rather a national
than a private concern, a little attention to the
effect of this interference, may ferve to correct
the miftake.

A candid and faithful hiftory of religious inftitutions, is a grand defideratum in litera-
ture; and its effect would infallibly be, to
excite in the mind of the liberal enquirer, either
contempt or indignation, againft every fect and
party, without exception. In order to appreciate
the value of ecclefiaftical eftablifhments, we muft
recollect, that to the tyranny of priefts we are indebted, for the flow progrefs of truth, in religion,
in philofophy, and in civil government: their

D 3   dread

dread of innovation, and their earneft folicitude
to perpetuate the empire of ignorance and fuperftition, having uniformly excited them to oppofe
every generous attempt to promote the diffufion
of knowledge amongft mankind. That *alliance
between church and ftate*, which has almoft every
where been formed for the vile purpofe of en-
flaving the world, has produced " acts for the
uniformity of worfhip," and " articles for the
taking away diverfity of opinion, and eftablifh-
ing one confent touching true religion :" and it
has enabled thofe who have arrogated to themfelves, the right of directing the confciences of the
reft of mankind, to dictate what opinions are to
be received or rejected, and what actions are to
be performed or avoided; and to enforce thofe
dictates, not only by the denunciation of eternal
damnation to the difobedient, which, if it were all,
would perhaps be pretty generally difregarded;
but alfo by that which comes nearer to every
man's feelings, by the terror of every fpecies of
temporal punifhment; by fines, confifcations, im-
prifonments, and death itfelf. Nor has it been
forgotten

forgotten in the midft of this " torrent, tempeft, and, as I may fay, whirlwind*" of holy zeal for the falvation of immortal fouls, to recommend in the moft glowing and animated language of appro- bation, that firft of all virtues, that effectual co- vering for the multitude of fins, that expiatory fa- crifice of fovereign efficacy, a liberal contribution of the good things of this life, towards fupport- ing the honour and dignity of holy church ! In this article the clergy of every fect, Heathen, Jewifh, Chriftian, and Mahometan are unani- mous; and it is in the fteady and uniform zeal with which this effential doctrine has been en- forced, that we are furnifhed with the cleareft proof of the truth of that trite obfervation, that " priefts of all religions are the fame."

Little however is done, or even attempted, by the national clergy in any part of the world, to- wards checking the progrefs of immorality ; and it is notorious, that in this country, the advantage derived to the caufe of virtue from the labours of

* Shakfpeare's Hamlet.

thefe

thefe fpiritual paftors and teachers, is altogether difproportionate to the enormous expence of the inftitution. Scarcely any attention whatever is paid to that moft important of all objects, the initiation of the young and ignorant, in the elements of religion and morality. The majority of the people do not frequent, either the authorifed places of public inftruction, or any other; and if they are withheld from attendance by a notion, that little advantage is to be derived from it, the opinion is rendered plaufible, by obferving the conduct of thofe whofe attendance is the moft regular.

This point deferves fome confideration; becaufe public preaching, or the delivery of formal difcourfes, as is the practice of the clergy, in the places appropriated to what is called public worfhip, is highly extolled, as the moft important mode of conveying religious and moral inftruction.

It is true indeed that, in general, the warmeft advocates for this practice have been divines; who, though it would be extremely uncandid to

fuggeft

fuggeft that they are always governed by interefted motives, may however, I think, very fairly be
fuppofed to be liable to fome portion of that profeffional bias, which is well known to prompt
even the beft and moft enlightened of mankind,
to overrate the value of thofe employments in
which themfelves are engaged*. From divines,
therefore, no impartial opinion upon the fubject
can be expected. We fhall do well to weigh
their arguments; but we muft not implicitly
truft to their affertions. We muft carefully examine the fubject for ourfelves. The importance
of the enquiry is fufficiently evident from this

---

* One learned profeffor goes fo far as to affert, that were
public worfhip and public inftruction interrupted for a confiderable time, men would lofe all fenfe of religion, run wild,
prey upon one another, and *foon* became little better than the
favages. *Credat Judacus!* Leechman's Serm. Vol. I. Serm.
X. Had this good man been a dancing-mafter inftead of a
divine, he might have *imagined*, but it would not have been in
his way to *write*, that were dancing fchools difcontinued, men
would lofe their erect pofture, go on all fours, and foon become little better than the Orang-Outang. In the vaft empire
of China, however, there is neither ftate-religion, nor public
inftruction; yet the conduct of the people is more orderly and
moral than that of Europeans. Whether there are any danc-
ing-mafters, I know not.

fingle

fingle confideration; that the utility of preaching, is made an argument for the neceffity of an
order of men, which, if it cannot be proved to be
highly ferviceable, ought, for many reafons be-
fides the vaft expence of fupporting it, to be
wholly laid afide *. Let us then, as fairly as we
can, for in vain fhall we hope to be entirely
emancipated from prejudice, endeavour to eftimate the value of this practice.

Were we to indulge in conjecture on the probable advantages of preaching, before enquiry
into its actual effect, our expectation would not
be much raifed by obferving, in what manner the
office of the miniftry is ufually acquired.

The emoluments of a richly endowed church,
like that of England, are confidered as a fpecies
of property; and are purchafed, like other property, as a provifion for children. When young
men, therefore, receive ordination, and fubfcribe
their *unfeigned affent and confent* to articles which

---

* Voltaire, fomewhere remarks, in his lively way—"If
England had feventy thoufand priefts, inftead of feventy
thoufand failors, what a different figure would fhe make in
Europe!"

they

they *do not believe,* for this reafon only, that the property which they are deftined to enjoy, cannot be held upon any other terms, is it to be expected that they will pay any greater attention to the duties attached to the facred character, than what is exacted from them by law? Will they not, on the contrary, be heartily difpofed to confider thofe duties, as fo many burthens and in · cumbrances, which it is their bufinefs to make as light as poffible? Can it be fuppofed that they will make any facrifice of thofe fafhionable, though immoral, purfuits and amufements to which they think themfelves by their fortune entitled, in order to " give themfelves wholly" to religion, to " do the work of an evangelift," to be " examples of the believers, in word, in converfation, in charity, in fpirit, in faith, in purity * ?" Are genuine religion and found morals likely to derive much fupport from thofe flimfy difcourfes which, for the fake of decency, they occafionally take the trouble to deliver? Is

* 1 Tim. iv. 12.

the

the great work of reformation to be expected from fuch hands?

With refpect to the higher offices of religion, by which fhe is enabled to " lift her mitred front in courts and parliaments * ;" not to mention that thefe diftinctions are too often obtained by the moft abject flattery of the great, or the moft fervile compliance with the corrupt politics of a court; it is well known, that the enjoyment of them is rarely found to confift with much anxiety for inftruction, either public or private. To be " apt to teach †," whatever might be the cafe in the age of primitive chriftianity, is as little the characteriftic of modern bifhops, as of any clafs of men whatever. If they teach any thing, it is the wholefome doctrine of fubmiffion to whatever our ecclefiaftical or civil governors fhall be pleafed to enjoin.

The clergy among the Diffenters are upon a very different footing. That profound refpect,

* Burke on the French Revolution.   † 2 Tim. ii. 24.

which

which was formerly paid to them by their adherents, has been long decreasing; and few of them, in the present day, possess any considerable portion of that authority which is so flattering to the pride of human nature. Nor are there any temptations held out to avarice or ambition, from honours or emoluments. The salary of the most fortunate dissenting minister, will scarcely equal that of a reputable merchant's clerk; while the stipend of others is inferior to the wages of a bricklayer's labourer; and their condition, upon the whole, not more enviable than that of the poorest Welch curate. Still, however, various causes concur to furnish a succession of ministers. Sometimes, the mistaken piety of a parent determines the fate of his unfortunate son, and sometimes, his vanity. For the minister, though often obliged to " bear the proud man's contumely," and to " duck his learned pate to the golden fool," is always, in some sort, considered as a gentleman. In a few instances it has happened, that a lad at school, having made an extraordinary proficiency in the classics, has for that

reason

reafon alone been devoted to the facred office: as if an unfortunate difpofition to learn languages could poffibly merit fo fevere a punifhment, as the being condemned to fubfift for life, upon forty pounds a year. Thus, from the operation of various circumftances, are boys fclected, fometimes before their talents or difpofitions can be known, and fometimes in defiance of every indication of nature, to be educated for the miniftry.

After having finifhed their preparatory ftudies, their object is, to be chofen by fome church or congregation, as paftor, or affiftant preacher. In this fituation, what is their bufinefs? Is it to affift their hearers in their enquiries after truth? No fuch thing! It is to maintain a fyftem of opinions which is the ftandard of orthodoxy in that particular connexion. In order to this, it is expected, that at a certain ceremony called ordination, to which many fuperftitious ideas are ufually annexed, they fhould make a full confeffion and declaration, of whatever they believe. or difbelieve. In the performance of this duty, they are carefully watched by every old woman

of

of both fexes in the congregation; and the probable confequence of any confiderable departure
from the faith, is either a divifion of the fociety,
or the rejection of the minifter *.

Shall we then wonder that they often enter
upon the exercife of their profeffion with a heavy
heart;—that they perform the fuppofed duties of
it without fpirit or energy, and with little profit
to the hearers;—that many aukwardly endeavour
to conceal their fentiments, or to accommodate
them to the tafte of their employers;—or that in
an age which begins to think for itfelf, and to

---

* This tyranny is not univerfal. The public worfhip at the
chapel in Effex-ftreet, for inftance, has little fimilarity to the
general ftate of things amongft the diffenters. Its truly apof-
tolic founder feems to have been as perfectly unfettered by
creeds and fyftems as any of the philofophers of antiquity.
Like them he opened his fchool of morals and religion, and
invited the world to attend his lectures. Thofe who were fo
happy as to accept the invitation, liftened to difcourfes which,
for their importance, might have claimed the attention of a
Locke or a Newton, and for their fimplicity might have been
addreffed to children. His fucceffor too has great merit.
Yet this inftitution will degenerate. The truftees of the
building will at length become truftees of the faith; and future minifters will be chofen, as in other diffenting congregations, to teach whatever they, in their wifdom or their ignorance, fhall have pre-ordained to be taught.

think

think freely, not a few fhould dare to break the fetters of prejudice, and to efcape from a fituation which prefents fo little profpect of either profit, honour, or ufefulnefs?

But, whatever may be the character or fituation of the minifters of this or that denomination, or however objectionable the particular conftitution of any ecclefiaftical eftablifhment, ftill it is triumphantly infifted upon, that the moral and religious conduct of thofe who ftatedly attend upon public inftruction, is a fufficient proof of its utility. A practice, it is faid, which is followed by fuch happy confequences muft be highly deferving of encouragement; and " the " advantage of having the moft falutary inftruc- " tions on every part of human duty enforced " by the moft powerful confiderations, laid be- " fore whole affemblies at once," is manifeft and undeniable.

This triumph, however, if we miftake not, is premature.

Should we even admit, what may perhaps be true, that the delivery of public lectures to large audiences

audiences had its ufes, and was entitled to encouragement, in an age when books were fcarce
and coftly, and learning was confined to a very
fmall number of perfons; it would by no means
follow, that this practice ought ftill to be continued. It muft always have had its inconveni-
encies and its dangers. Public orations are eafily
capable of being made the inftruments of incal-
culable mifchief. They may be directed to in-
flame the imagination, without enlightening the
mind; to roufe the paffions, without informing
the judgment. A more dangerous character can
hardly be imagined than an eloquent ecclefiaftic,
furrounded by an ignorant multitude, who have
been taught to confider him as an oracle. It
muft always therefore have been defirable, that
this mode of inftruction fhould be fuperfeded, by
fomething more certain in its effect, and lefs liable
to be abufed.

The INVENTION OF PRINTING has fupplied this
defideratum. By means of this nobleft of the mechanic arts, books are fo eafily multiplied, as to be
within the reach of the mafs of mankind; and

E

reading

reading will, at no great diftance of time, be univerfal. The advantages of this method of ac-
quiring knowledge, and its fuperiority to oral
inftruction, are fo manifeft, as fcarcely to need being pointed out. The lecture of the public orator is extremely liable to be mifunderftood, and
is not eafily retained; but what is written remains. He who is in poffeffion of a book, may,
after having read and confidered it, confult it
again and again, and return to it at any diftance
of time for frefh inftruction. In this way he is
enabled calmly to contemplate the fubject of his
enquiry in every poffible point of view; to de-
tect the various errors into which he may inad-
vertently or haftily have fallen; to review even
his own lateft decifions, and to correct his ma-
tureft judgment by the difcoveries of others. The
progrefs of truth, therefore, is much more likely
to be affifted by books, than by *viva voce* difcourfes: and if I were called upon to mention
that event in hiftory which is, without exception,
and beyond all comparifon, moft interefting to
mankind, I fhould not hefitate to name the IN-

VENTION

VENTION OF PRINTING. It is this omnipotent engine which is deftined to move the world; to renovate the face of nature; to change the afpect of human affairs. The powers that be, have indeed taken alarm at its effects; and in more than one country of Europe, violent efforts are even now making to annihilate its exiftence, or to confine its operations. But no combination of partial interefts fhall be able to arreft its wonder-working progrefs, or to extinguifh that light which it has already diffufed over the earth. It will fhine more and more unto the perfect day. Every cloud of ignorance, error, and fuperftition, fhall at length vanifh before it; and human nature, having attained a maturity, phyfical, intellectual, and moral, hitherto unknown, fhall acknowledge that, under Providence, it is indebted for its nobleft improvements, its fublimeft difcoveries, and its fweeteft enjoyments, to the INVENTION OF PRINTING.

Should we farther admit, for the fake of argument, and it is only in this view that it can be admitted, that the conduct of ftated hearers is in

E 2

general

general exemplary, ftill it remains to be proved, that this good conduct is the effect of preaching. No error is more common than to confound caufes and effects, and to miftake the one for the other.

A confcientious man will fteadily conform to whatever he conceives to be his *duty*, and avoid the contrary. Whether this belief be the effect of free enquiry, or of early prejudice; whether he be a philofopher or a bigot, a Gentoo or a Chriftian, a difciple of Confucius or of Swedenborg, it is ftill the fame. As a man of principle, his practice will be uniformly governed by his fenfe of right and wrong. And if he have been told from his youth, that he ought to attend upon religious ordinances, if not for his own fake, yet as an example to others, his attendance will infallibly be regular and punctual, even though, inftead of deriving any benefit from it, he fhould find it, as muft often be the cafe, a fevere trial of his patience. It is indeed not eafy to conceive, how any man of fenfe can prevail upon himfelf regularly to endure the extreme dullnefs and ab-

3   furdity

furdity of fome of our pulpits, who has not had the misfortune to be taught in early life, that he is thereby *performing a duty*, which he cannot omit without incurring the difpleafure of Heaven. But under the influence of this idea, the fevereft penance may be cheerfully fupported; and thus a regular attendance upon fermons and prayers may be the *effect*, and not the *caufe*, of a virtuous difpofition *.

Is

* I know not how it happens, but it is a fact, that many of our pulpit orators offer to their adult hearers fuch miferable trafh as they would be perfectly afhamed to addrefs to children. Ufelefs and unintelligible jargon, it feems, will do for men and women, but when we inftruct children, we muft talk common fenfe—I remember, many years ago, being led by curiofity to a chapel occupied by the Moravian brethren in Fetter-lane. In the whole courfe of the fervice, confifting of prayer, finging, and preaching, little occurred from which I could derive either pleafure or profit. Almoft every thing that was not abfolutely incomprehenfible, appeared to me highly abfurd. On the breaking up of the affembly a few perfons remained ; and, wifhing to fee and hear every thing, I remained alfo. The preacher defcended from the pulpit, and feating himfelf at a fmall table, near which were collected twenty or thirty children, from five to ten years of age, he addreffed them on the leading points of natural and fupernatural religion, in a fhort difcourfe, fo fimple, familiar, and intelligible in point of ftyle, and fo rational and important as to the matter; in a word, fo completely the reverfe of every thing I had

E 3

been

Is it, however, in fact, true, that the moral conduct of thofe who attend upon public inftruction,
is fo much fuperior to that of the reft of the
world, as they would have us believe? This
point ought not to be haftily conceded. Do
we find nothing of envy, hatred, malice, or un-
charitablenefs, amongft the members of what are
called chriftian churches? Is there nothing like
fpiritual pride, or hypocrify, in any of thefe focieties? To fpeak plainly, are they not the very
hot-beds in which thofe vices are infallibly produced? It is perhaps true, that the difcipline
of the fectaries may be fome reftraint upon the
members of their little congregations, fo far as
relates to the more grofs and open inftances of
immorality; but who, that has any acquaintance with the management of parifhes, ever per-
ceived, that the moft regular attendance upon
the religious ordinances of the church of England, had any effect towards preventing a church-

been hearing for near two hours, as to excite in my mind the
utmoft furprife and aftonifhment! Why could not he have
talked thus fenfibly to the fathers and mothers?

warden

warden or an overfeer, to fay nothing of the par-
fon or the clerk, from enjoying the obfcene toaft,
vociferating the profane oath, or getting drunk
at a vifitation dinner? On the other hand, have
we not often occafion to notice the warmeft bene-
volence, and the moft irreproachable integrity, in
thofe who profefs no attachment to external and
ceremonious obfervances, and who confider the
prieftly office as entirely fuperfluous?

Nothing in fact can be more clearly evident,
than that thofe good difpofitions which, where-
ever they exift, contribute fo much to the comfort of focial life, are the fruit, not of pulpit
oratory, but of that patient and unremitting attention to reproof and exhortation, which is peculiar to the natural and endearing connexion of
private families. Public oratory has nothing in
its nature fuitable to this end. It may indeed,
fometimes, produce aftonifhing effects, by roufing
the paffions, or fwaying the judgment of the
multitude, in favour of any object of the moment, whether good or bad, of which very memorable inftances are recorded in hiftory; but it

is utterly incapable of implanting in the mind, the feeds of moral fentiment; of inftilling the firft principles of generous and manly conduct; or of producing that fteady and uniform charac- ter of virtue, which, happily for the world, is fo often the effect of a long-continued courfe of fa- mily difcipline.

It is not denied, that hitherto the greater num- ber of ferious chriftians have been frequenters of public worfhip, and public inftruction. But the developement of error and fuperftition is flow and gradual. There was a time when almoft all chriftians believed the doctrine of tranfubftan- tiation, now fo juftly exploded. As free enquiry proceeds—and no violence will be able to fup- prefs it—it may come to pafs, that religious ce- remonies and profeffional difcourfes fhall be no more valued by the thinking part of mankind, nor have any more connexion with virtuous con- duct, than extreme unction, or papal abfolution, have at prefent.

This way of arguing from the fuppofed effects of opinions, muft indeed be confeffed to open a

door

door to uncandid fuggeftion, and fallacious in-
ference. It is eafy to fay, " I am holier than
thou;" but mere confident affertion, can furnifh
no proof of any thing, but the pride or the impu-
dence of him who reforts to it; and it would be
for the honour of all religious perfuafions, to
pay more regard to the apoftolical advice, " not
to think of themfelves more highly than they
ought to think," inftead of indulging that party
fpirit, which prompts men to view with contempt,
or hatred, the characters and perfons of thofe
whom they choofe to call their adverfaries *.—
Thus much, however, may, I think, be fafely af-
firmed—that public inftruction and public worfhip, confidered as expedients for diffufing religious knowlege and promoting moral practice, have completely failed. Nor is it probable,
that if thefe inftitutions were utterly unknown,
there would exift more vice and profligacy of

* This however is the argument adopted by Andrew Fuller
in his celebrated treatife entitled *Calviniftic and Socinian Syftems
compared.* We Calvinifts are better men than you Arians and
Socinians: therefore Calvinifm is the truth! Very conclufive,
no doubt, if we admit the premifes; and for thefe, we have the
modeft gentleman's own word.

every kind, public and private, or lefs of the
peaceable and humble fpirit of chriftianity, than
are now to be found in this country, where religion, or rather what is commonly but undeferv-
edly called religion, is fupported at an annual
expence of at leaft five millions fterling.

That religion and morals were ever the real
objects of thefe inftitutions, is indeed extremely
queftionable. It is certain in many inftances, and
highly credible in others, that thofe who have
been moft active in promoting the eftablifhment
of church authority, have regarded it merely as an
engine of ftate, happily adapted to curb the licen-
tioufnefs of the people, and to ftrengthen the
hands of government. Nor have they ever been
difappointed, except when the intereft of the
church has been imprudently neglected. While
kings have manifefted a difpofition to be "nurfing fathers" and queens " nurfing mothers" to
the church, a great majority of the facred order
have always been ready on their part, without
fcruple to diffeminate, and to " enforce by the
moft *powerful* confiderations," whatever doctrines
were

were underftood to be agreeable to the monarch.
In the courfe of this dishonourable employment
every moral precept of chriftianity has been trod-
den under foot, by thofe who have claimed to be
the depofitaries of its facred myfteries; and the
pretended advocates of order, morality, and religion, by the fupport they have afforded to tyranny, and the oppofition they have made to the
progrefs of knowlege, have, in reality, been the
greateft enemies of all the three.

Very far is it from my intention to affert, that this
defcription applies univerfally to every minifter
of religion. There are, no doubt, many illuftrious exceptions; fome of whom, I have the honour to count amongft the number of my friends.
It is, however, the direct tendency of the profeffion to produce this character; and it is a fact,
that divines, for the moft part, whether in or out
of the eftablifhment, have ever been unfriendly
to *real* liberty; thofe of the favoured faction, by
their domineering temper, and thofe of the op-
preffed or tolerated fects, by their abject and
cringing fervility, having eminently contributed

4   to

to deprefs the fpirit of freedom, and to check the progrefs of human intellect. The latter have incurred a double difgrace; for while, on the one hand, they have meanly fubmitted to flatter the power which permitted them to exift, they have, on the other, attempted to exercife the fame fpiritual tyranny over their tame adherents, which they condemned in their triumphant adverfaries.

Upon the whole, if wifdom may be collected from experience, if we may prefume to judge of the future from the paft, we are abundantly warranted in predicting, that while mankind are influenced by that fyftem which fuppofes it neceffary for the people to be inftructed in their religious and moral obligations, by perfons claiming a divine commiffion, and expecting to be gratified with ample falaries and poffeffions, as the reward of their fuppofed fervices; in a word, while religion continues to be a trade, and there are priefts who can fay, " by this craft we have our wealth," fo long will the prevalence of genuine liberty and pure religion be utterly hopelefs.

To

To DOMESTIC INSTRUCTION then, aided by the noble art of printing, we muſt look for the cultivation of the beſt principles of the human mind. And though the conduct of the prieſt-hood in all ages, if any credit be due to hiſtory, cannot but have had the moſt unhappy influence in counteracting and weakening its effect; yet ſtill to domeſtic inſtruction we are chiefly indebted, for whatever of excellence exiſts in the human cha-racter. That much of excellence *does* exiſt, and that ſtill more is *capable* of exiſting, are poſitions which can hardly be doubted by any but the wildeſt enthuſiaſt. But perfection is only to be attained by ſlow and gradual advances; and the moral improvement of our race cannot be ex-pected to make any conſiderable progreſs, till ſu-perſtition ſhall have loſt its hold on the human mind; till all pretences to ſacredneſs of charac-ter ſhall be laid aſide; till knowledge ſhall be ge-nerally diffuſed, and EVERY PARENT SHALL BE THE INSTRUCTOR OF HIS OWN OFFSPRING.

PART III.

ON CHRISTIANITY AS A SUPERNATURAL COMMUNICATION.

Of the great fubjects of human enquiry, Religion, if it have any foundation at all, muft be the moft important. No queftion more interefting to an intelligent being can be afked, than the following—What are my obligations, confidered as the fubject of a moral governor, and the expectant of an endlefs life? Nor can any refearches be more worthy of our rational powers, than fuch as relate to fo glorious an expectation. Whatever promifes to afford any additional light on this momentous fubject, excites our curiofity; and if the communication profeffes to be fupernatural, it immediately claims our moft attentive regard.

To fupernatural authority the pretenfions have

been

been numerous; but it is certain that they have not been all valid, nor equally fuccefsful. In this quarter of the world, chriftianity, being generally received, and the profeffion of it enforced by law, would on that account, if on no other, be entitled to our principal attention. It is not, however, agreed in what it confifts. A very great variety of reprefentations of its nature and importance have been given, by the different fects and parties of its profeffors.

Some fay it is founded on an event called, the fall of man ; that is, a tranfgreffion of the firft created man, whom they reprefent as the covenant head of his future race, and as having, by a fingle act of difobedience, entailed everlafting mifery on himfelf and all his pofterity; which confequence they fay would certainly have taken place, had not a very benevolent being, whom they call the fecond perfon in the Trinity, and the creator of all worlds, condefcended to be born of a woman, and to fuffer death, in order to appeafe the wrath, or fatisfy the juftice, of the firft perfon in this Trinity, who is reprefented as otherwife,

otherwife, relentlcfs and implacable *. A grett majority of the abettors of this fyftem hold, that while on earth he appointed certain authoritative teachers of his doctrine, who ordained others in fucceffion down to this day; whofe decrees on the fubject of religion are binding upon the people wherever chriflianity is received †.

Other reprefentations of chriftianity have been given, in infinite variety. Only one more fhall be here noticed ; namely, that which fpeaks of Jefus as a mere human being, but diftinguifhed

* The pious Dr. Watts appears to have confidered it as the glory of our holy religion, that it contains more of the *marvellous* than the heathen mythology, or the tales of knight-errantry. " There is nothing amongft all the ancient *fables* or later " *romances*," fays he, " that have two fuch *extremes* united in " them, as the eternal God becoming an infant of days ; the " poffeffor of the palace of heaven laid to fleep in a manger; " the holy Jefus, who knew no fin, bearing the fins of men in " his body on the tree ; agonies of forrow loading the foul of " him who was God over all, bleffed for ever ; and the fo- " vereign of life ftretching his arms on a crofs, bleeding, and " expiring." WATTS. Preface to Lyric Poems.

Thefe he thinks are admirable fubjects for poetry, which delights in *ftrange things!* A more fevere fatire on chriftianity was never pronounced by its bittereft enemy!

† The church hath power to decree rites or ceremonies, and authority in controverfies of faith. Art. 20, of the church of England.

from

from the whole race by larger fupernatural communications than had ever before been afforded
to any man ; by virtue of which he became the
legiflator of a new difpenfation, and the deftined judge of all mankind at the day of final
retribution.   In addition to which, it has of late
been ftrongly infifted upon, and perhaps only of
late, by any perfons calling themfelves chriftians,
that natural religion affords no intimation of a
future life, and that we are indebted for all our
information on this fubject to the chriftian doctrine of a refurrection from the dead *.

Nor are the profeffors of chriftianity lefs divided on the fubject of the proper evidences of its

* This appears to be a fundamental article in the fyftem of
that great ornament of human nature, the venerable Dr. Prieftley. It would be endlefs to note the paffages of his voluminous
writings, in which the doctrine is afferted, or implied.   He is
confequently obliged to maintain, without the leaft fhadow of
proof, and, fo far as I can perceive, in defiance of every thing
that can be called probability, that the belief of a future ftate,
amongft the ancient heathens, muft, fomehow or other, have
been derived by *tradition* from the immediate defcendants of
Noah; yet the Jews, judging from their own hiftory,
appear to have been lefs acquainted with it than any other nation of antiquity.

F   truth,

truth, than concerning its nature and importance. By vaſt numbers it is held, that the authority of the CHURCH above mentioned, which they ſay has ſubſiſted in a ſucceſſion of biſhops from the times of the apoſtles, is our proper and ſufficient warrant for the reception of chriſtianity in general, as well as our only ſafe guide with reſpect to every particular tenet and opinion—while others no leſs confidently maintain, that we muſt take both the evidence and the doctrines of our religion from the books of the New Teſtament; and that the hiſtories therein contained of MI-. RACLES ſaid to have been performed by the firſt promulgators of chriſtianity, afford an adequate ground and reaſon to all ſucceeding ages, for the acknowledgment of the divine miſſion of Jeſus, and for ſubmiſſion to his authority.

The examination of the ſyſtem which refers the credibility of the chriſtian religion, and the deciſion of all controverſies concerning it, to church authority, is not directly intended in the preſent eſſay; the principal object of which is, to enquire in as ſhort a compaſs as poſſible, or rather to lead the

the reader to enquire, into the nature and importance of miraculous evidence.

With this view, I fhall fimply ftate the fub-
ftance of a late converfation on the fubject with
a very intelligent friend; and, without a fingle
additional remark, fhall leave it to the confideration of the candid reader.

We had been hearing an elaborate difcourfe on
the refurrection of Jefus; in which the preacher
infifted ftrongly on the indubitable *certainty* of
the fact, and on the *truth* of the doctrines of
chriftianity as a direct and neceffary *confequence*.
We both admired the ingenuity of the orator,
and had no reafon to diftruft his honefty; but we
were, neither of us, completely fatisfied with his
reafoning: and fome hints which I threw out to
this effect, drew from my friend the following
obfervations, which I thought of fufficient importance to commit to writing.

" That a miracle, cannot even to the immediate
" fpectator, prove any doctrine to be *true*, which
" is already by other evidence known to be *falfe*,

F 2   " is

" is clear, not only becaufe no pofition can be
" true and falfe at the fame time; but alfo, be-
" caufe in this cafe, it would be much more pro-
" bable, that the performer had ingenioufly con-
" trived to deceive the eyes of the fpectator, than
" that the one God had furnifhed him with the
" power to work a real miracle, for the mere
" purpofe of confounding and perplexing the un-
" derftandings of his creatures.   This will be ftill
" more ftrikingly evident if the doctrine in quef-
" tion be of a moral nature.   Let us fuppofe, for
" inftance, an attempt to prove that envy, ha-
" tred, and malice, are, in their nature and con-
" fequences, preferable to candour and benevo-
" lence; and that fomething like a miracle
" fhould be wrought in fupport of it—Would
" not every underftanding revolt at the abfur-
" dity; and would not the pretended miracle be
" inftantly rejected as an impofture?

" On the other hand, to produce the evidence
" of miracles in proof of that which is already
" fufficiently known and underftood, is mani-
" feftly fuperfluous.   What, for example, could
                                    " a miracle

" a miracle do towards proving that parents
" ought take care of their young children, or
" that children ought to obey their parents; du-
" ties which, arifing immediately out of the re-
" lative fituation of the parties, are clear and
" obvious by the light of nature? Or if the
" object be to inculcate on fociety the love
" of truth, as more conducive to general happi-
" nefs than deceit and falfehood, how can it be
" imagined that fo plain a doctrine can be made
" plainer by the exhibition of any miracle*?"

" If

---

* How divinely does Cicero exprefs himfelf to this purpofe!
Eft quidem vera lex, RECTA RATIO, naturæ congruens, diffufa
in omnes, conftans, fempiterna; quæ vocet ad officium jubendo, vetando a fraude deterreat; quæ tamen nec probos fruftra
jubet aut vetat, nec improbos jubendo aut vetando movet.
Huic legi nec obrogari fas eft, neque derogari ex hac aliquid
licet, neque tota abrogari poteft. Nec vero aut per fenatum
aut per populum folvi hac lege poffumus. Neque eft quæren-
dus explanator, aut interpres ejus alius. Nec erit alia lex Ro-
mæ, alia Athenis; alia nunc, alia pofthac; fed et omnes gen-
tes, et omni tempore, una lex, et fempiterna et immortalis con-
tinebit. Uuufque erit communis quafi magifter et imperator
omnium, DEUS ille, legis hujus inventor, deceptator, lator;
cui non parebit, ipfe fe fugiet, ac naturam hominis afperna-
bitur: atque hoc ipfo luet maximas pœnas, etiam fi cætera
fupplicia, quæ putantur, effugerit. FRAG. DE REPUB. Lib. iii.

Right reafon is a true law; agreeable to nature, univerfal,

invariable,

" If this be the cafe with refpect to the imme-
" diate fpectator, it feems not eafy to imagine what
" can be the direct ufe of a miracle to one who
" has no perfonal knowledge of its reality, but de-
" rives all his information concerning it from the
" report of others.   Let us fuppofe fuch a man to
" be told, that two thoufand years ago, a perfon
" profeffing to be divinely infpired had taught the
" doctrine of an univerfal Providence; and had
" fupported his pretenfions, and confirmed his

invariable, eternal ; which invites men to duty by precepts,
and deters them from inquiry by prohibitions; and which
never commands or prohibits the virtuous in vain, though the
wicked are unmoved by menaces or injunctions. Of this law
nothing can be changed or altered ; nor can the whole, or any
part of it, be repealed or cancelled.   No authority, either of
the fenate or the people, can releafe men from its obligation.
It is fo plain as to need no commentator or interpreter.   Nor is
it one law at Rome, another at Athens; one at this time, another hereafter; but the fame eternal and immortal law muft
bind all nations and all ages, under the controul of one prefid-
ing and directing power, even GOD himfelf, by whom this
law was contrived, adjufted, and eftablifhed; to which whoever refufes obedience muft fly from himfelf, and caft off the
nature of a man; and this he cannot do without fuffering the
fevereft tortures, though he fhould efcape thofe punifhments
which are commonly believed.

                                        " teachings,

" teachings, by a difplay of miraculous power—
" Would it be reafonable for him to engage in a
" tedious, and perhaps finally unfuccefsful en-
" quiry, concerning the reality of this perfon's
" divine miffion; to examine the miracles re-
" corded in hiftory, and the alledged circumftance
" of their having been wrought in confirmation
" of this particular doɛtrine; to undertake all
" this labour, with a view—to what? to obtain
" fatisfaɛtion concerning a doɛtrine, the truth
" of which may at any time be fhewn by a few
" plain arguments! Or fhould the matter in
" queftion be lefs fimple and obvious than that
" above mentioned; fhould even the procefs of
" enquiry, upon the principles of reafon, have its
" difficulties, and the refult be fomewhat uncer-
" tain; ftill, furely, in no cafe, can either the
" difficulty or uncertainty be fo great as that
" which attends the inveftigation of ancient
" writings, in order, if poffible, to afcertain
" their genuinenefs, authenticity, and meaning,
" and the truth of the faɛts recorded in them;

" than

" than which no enquiry can be more tedious
" and intricate, and, for the moſt part, no labour
" more fruitleſs and unprofitable. In all caſes,
" therefore, in which human nature can feel an
" intereſt, would it not be much more eaſy to
" learn the truth, independently of the miracle,
" than to arrive at *abſolute certainty* concerning
" the miracle, in order to prove the doctrine?
" I ſay abſolute certainty, becauſe nothing ſhort
" of this can be of any uſe in the caſe we are
" confidering. The hiſtory of a miracle which
" *may be either true or falſe,* may afford ſome
" amuſement, and even ſome inſtruction; but
" cannot without abſurdity be admitted as evi-
" dence of the truth of any doctrine, ſince it can-
" not communicate that *certainty* which it does
" not poſſefs."

Here, though I love to hear my friend talk, I
could no longer forbear to interrupt him.—" If
this be the caſe," ſaid I; " if hiſtories of miracles
alledged to have been wrought in ancient times,
thoſe of the Goſpel for example, muſt not be
                                        confidered

confidered as proofs of its doctrines, what have we to do with them? Why not reject them altogether?"

" This is the very point to which I was com-
" ing," replied my friend; " and I think the
" anfwer to your queftion is not difficult."—

" That the miraculous facts, which are faid to
" have accompanied the firft preaching of chrif-
" tianity, *are not of any great direct importance to*
" *us* at this day, does indeed follow from what
" I have been faying ; but that they ought, there-
" fore, to be utterly rejected as *falfe*, is fo far from
" being a legitimate confequence of our reafon-
" ing, that, on the contrary, I have no hefitation
" in afferting, that the lefs we feel ourfelves inte-
" refted in the facts recorded, the more eafily may
" we acquiefce in the truth of the narration.

" We all believe many things, of which we nei-
" ther have, nor can have, any abfolute certainty.
" This, indeed, is the cafe of univerfal hiftory.
" When I read in an ancient writer, it matters
" not whether poet or hiftorian, that the Greeks
" waged

" waged a ten years war againft Troy; having
" no poffible motive to difpute the fact, I admit
" it without hefitation.   But if any man could
" perfuade me, that my eternal falvation were
" depending upon its truth, he would, at the
" fame time, fill my mind with doubt and anx-
" iety.   I fhould fly for relief to the perufal of
" every thing that has been written concerning
" this famous tranfaction, but fhould probably
" never obtain it, fo long as I fhould continue to
" imagine the fubject to be of great importance
" to me.   If once, however, I fhould be fo hap-
" py as to difcard this groundlefs notion, I fhould
" recover my wonted tranquillity, and fhould be-
" lieve the ftory.

    " In like manner, the miraculous facts record-
" ed in the Gofpel may be received as hiftory,
" although, not being attended with indifputable
" certainty, they cannot be confidered as prov-
" ing the truth of doctrines with which they do
" not appear to have any neceffary connexion.
" And if we be convinced of the fupernatural
                                          " origin

" origin of chriftianity *upon other grounds,* we
" fhall perhaps think it not improbable that an
" extraordinary difplay of divine power might
" accompany its firft preaching; efpecially if we
" can perceive any valuable end to be *then* an-
" fwered by it; and confequently may believe
" the miracles of the Gofpel, although they
" fhould be of no immediate and direct ufe to
" ourfelves.

" Now, I think, whoever attentively confiders
" the earlieft records of chriftianity, muft be
" ftruck with one very remarkable and indifput-
" able fact; which feems to fhew, that it could
" be no other than a fupernatural communica-
" tion; although it teaches nothing that is not
" perfectly agreeable to human reafon, and per-
" haps nothing of great importance which is not
" naturally difcoverable by it; and although all
" its leading doctrines may be collected from
" the writings of heathen philofophers, who, fo
" far as we know, had no other guide than the
" light of nature. The fact I mean is, that THE

" CLEARNESS,

" CLEARNESS, CONSISTENCY, COMPREHENSION,
" AND SUBLIMITY, OF THE SYSTEM OF DOC-
" TRINE CONTAINED IN THE NEW TESTAMENT,
" DEMONSTRATE A KNOWLEDGE OF THE IM-
" PORTANT SUBJECTS OF WHICH IT TREATS,
" ALTOGETHER DISPROPORTIONATE TO THE
" NATURAL MEANS OF INFORMATION POS-
" SESSED BY THE WRITERS; AND INFINITE-
" LY SURPASSING THE ACTUAL NATURAL AT-
" TAINMENTS OF THE HUMAN MIND, IN ANY
" PRECEDING OR SUBSEQUENT AGE, IN ANY
" PART OF THE HABITABLE GLOBE.

" The fages of ancient Greece, fmit with the
" love of fcience, neglected no means of ac-
" quiring knowledge; travelled into remote re-
" gions in fearch of inftruction from men and
" books, and devoted their lives to the ftudy of
" philofophy. Such of their writings as have
" efcaped the deftroying hand of time, and the
" ravages of gothic ignorance, difcover an ardour
" in the purfuit of truth, a perfevering atten-
" tion to the cultivation of the intellectual powers,

" and

" and an indefatigable patience in the inveſtiga-
" tion of the moſt interefting ſubjeŭts of human
" enquiry, which muſt for ever command the
" admiration of mankind. They abound in fine
" obſervations on life and manners, and in the moſt
" dignified ſentiments of moral virtue. But they
" abound alſo in errors and in doubts. Their
" authors differed from each other, and from
" themſelves, on many important points of hu-
" man conduŭt, and they were ftill leſs agreed
" on the intereſting ſubjeŭt of future expeŭta-
" tions.

" The teacher of Nazareth, on the other hand,
" and his humble followers, were very far from
" being in favourable circumſtances for the ac-
" quiſition of knowledge. They were chiefly
" men of low circumſtances, of mean em-
" ployments, and without education. Jeſus him-
" ſelf was the ſon of a poor carpenter, and pro-
" bably worked many years with his father for
" his ſubſiſtence. We might be certain that he
" could read, if it had not been mentioned in
" his hiſtory, as that accompliſhment was uni-

l   " verſal

" verfal amongft his countrymen : but it is im-
" probable that he knew of any other books than
" thofe of the old Teftament; nor is there the
" leaft trace of his acquaintance with any thing
" that had been done for the improvement
" of the human mind in the heathen world.
" Yet from this obfcurity he fuddenly emerg-
" ed ' to be a light to the gentiles and to be
" for falvation to the ends of the earth *.'
" Deriving nothing from human inftruction, he
" furpaffed all the philofophers in knowledge;
" and delineated with a mafter-hand the whole
" fcience of morals and divinity.　Without affift-
" ance from the fchools, he ' fpake as never man
" fpake †;' and in eafy and familiar difcourfes
" delivered a fyftem of doctrine on the the tranf-
" cendently important fubjects of the govern-
" ment of God, and the duty and expectations of
" man, which is incapable of addition or im-
" provement, without error, and without de-
" fect.

　　" Every fact muft have its adequate caufe.

　　　* Acts xiii. 47.　　　† John vii. 46.

　　　　　　　　　　　　　　　　" How

" How then fhall we explain this fingular pheno-
" menon ?   How fhall we account for it, that a
" poor untutored carpenter, fhould not only have
" made fuch advances in religious and moral
" knowledge, as to have exceeded this or that
" philofopher, but fhould have been fo per-
" fectly mafter of thefe great fubjects, as to have
" furpaffed all the efforts of the wifeft and moft
" improved nations of the world ?   How, but by
" affenting to that which he himfelf uniformly
" declared,—that he derived not his knowledge
" from a human, but a fupernatural fource ?
" 'How knoweth this man letters,' faid the afto-
" nifhed Jews, ' having never learned !'   And
" what other folution of the difficulty can poffi-
" bly be offered, than that which proceeded from
" the mouth of the divine teacher himfelf?—' the
" doctrine is not mine, but his that fent me *.'

" If in this manner, by what is called internal
" evidence, it can be fatisfactorily made appear
" to us at this day, that chriftianity juftly lays
" claim to a fupernatural origin, and is thus pro-

* John vii. 15, 16.

" perly

" perly a miraculous difpenfation, it cannot fure-
" ly appear *prima facie* incredible, that its firft
" preaching fhould be attended with a vifible
" difplay of miraculous power. On the contrary,
" if it can be fhewn that fome important effect
" was to be *then* produced, fome valuable end
" to be *then* anfwered by this difplay, it may be
" admitted as an *hiftorical fact* without difficulty ;
" always remembering, that, like other hiftorical
" facts, the evidence of its truth depending upon
" *human teftimony*, can amount only to *probability*,
" and by no means to *certainty*."

" But what could that end be," exclaimed I
with eagernefs ? " You will oblige me by dif-
tinctly pointing it out."

" To that I have not the leaft objection," replied my friend, " if you have patience to hear
" me while I endeavour to ftate my idea of the
" defign of chriftianity itfelf; or to examine
" what were the circumftances on account of
" which it pleafed the fovereign Providence of
" heaven to raife up fo extraordinary a perfon as
" Jefus at that time."

I affured

I affured him this would add to my obligation, and he thus proceeded.

" Man, by the conftitution of that nature " which GOD has given him, is a moral and in- " telligent being; naturally furnifhed with the " means of difcovering the being and perfections " of Deity, the truths of moral obligation, and " a future ftate of rewards and punifhments; and " accordingly, *wherever there have been men,* in " proportion as their powers have been exerted, " thefe great truths have been more or lefs clearly " apprehended *.

" He

* The queftion whether religious and moral ideas are *na- tural,* has been the matter of very voluminous controverfy. But is not this a difpute about words, or, at moft, about a thing of no practical importance? If it be admitted on all hands, that men are fo conftituted and fo fituated, as neceffarily to become poffeffed of thefe ideas, though in very different de- grees of perfection, is it not idle to contend that they ought not to be called natural, becaufe infants are not born divines and moralifts? This mode of arguing would equally prove that teeth are not natural, becaufe we have them not at our birth ; or that walking is not natural, becaufe none walk but thofe who are taught; that is, the whole human race I Dif- putes fo frivolous may be kept *ad infinitum.* The following quotation exhibits the opinion of a man who had no opportu-

G   nity

" He has alfo animal appetites, implanted
" for wife purpofes; but when indulged to ex-
" cefs, tending to enfeeble the moral powers, to
" obfcure the light of truth, and to introduce
" into the mind confufion and mifery. This un-
" happy ftate of things has in fome degree or
" other taken place in all ages, and in every
" part of the world; but at certain periods, and
" in fome countries, the corruption of principles

nity of deriving any advantage from fupernatural revelation.
" Nulla gens tam fera, nemo omnium tam fit immanis, cujus
" mentem non imbuerit deorum opinio. Multi de diis prava
" fentiunt; id enim vitiofo more effici folet: omnes tamen
" effe vim et naturam divinam arbitrantur. Nec vero id col-
" licutio hominum aut confenfus efficit: non inftitutis opinio
" eft confirmata, non legibus. Omni autem in re confenfio
" ommium gentium, *lex naturæ* putanda eft."
No nation is fo barbarous, no human being fo favage, as to
be unacquainted with the idea of God. It muft be acknowledged, that many are led by the depraved ftate of their morals, to entertain very unworthy notions of their gods; but
ftill all believe in fome fuperior power. Nor is the origin of
this perfuafion to be traced to any combination or agree-
ment; nor its continuance to be afcribed to laws or eftablifhments; but in this, as in all other cafes, the univerfal confent of mankind muft be confidered as the *dictate of
nature.*

CIC. TUSCUL. I. 13.

" and

" and manners has been fo enormous, that it has
" pleafed Almighty God, in his great wifdom and
" mercy, to make ufe of extraordinary methods
" for producing a reformation. He may have
" done fo, in many inftances, in ages and coun-
" tries, with whofe hiftory we are either imper-
" fectly or not at all acquainted. For as the
" Creator of all minds muft neceffarily have con-
" tinual accefs to all, it is at leaft poffible, that
" fupernatural communications may have been
" more numerous than is commonly fuppofed.
" He may have been, for ought we can fay, the
" infpirer of thofe whom we are ufed to term Im-
" poftors; of Confucius, Mango-Capac, and Ma-
" homet. But we have much better information
" concerning that memorable inftance of his
" goodnefs to the world, the miffion of Jefus,
" and the fingular affiftance afforded to that ex-
" traordinary perfon, in his generous and emi-
" nently fuccefsful efforts to revive the dying
" caufe of religion and virtue; to turn men from
" darknefs to light, and from the power of Satan,

" or

" or corrupt and vicious difpofitions, to the fer-
" vice of God. The period in which this great
" perfon appeared was a very remarkable one ; it
" was a period of great knowledge in fome re-
" fpects, and of amazing ftupidity in others.
" The Roman empire was at its utmoft height,
" and the human fciences were cherifhed with
" ardour; while religion and morals, the moft
" important concerns of man, lay in a moft lan-
" guifhing and deplorable ftate. This wretched
" degeneracy is very accurately defcribed by the
" fine pen of the apoftle Paul, who, while he la-
" ments the corruption of the age, does not for-
" get to affert the *univerfality and fufficiency of na-*
" *tural religion,* in the cleareft terms ; afcribing
" all the evil, not to invincible ignorance, or
" original depravity, but to the criminal inatten-
" tion of mankind to the vifible appearances of
" Deity, in the works of his hands, and in the
" methods of his providence *.

" In order to effect a reformation, it was necef-

* Romans i.

" fary

" fary *to roufe men from this moral lethargy*, and to
" prevail upon them to *attend* to the voice of in-
" ftruction. By what method could this be done?
" By none, perhaps, fo fure and certain in its ef-
" fect, as by the public difplay of miraculous
" power. · The eyes of the moft ftupid of men
" would be naturally turned with admiration to-
" wards him, who could command the lame to
" walk, and the blind to fee; and he who could
" fatisfy the appetites of five or fix thoufand per-
" fons, with a few loaves of bread, could hardly
" fail to fecure five thoufand attentive hearers.
" In fhort, it appears to me, and if I am wrong, it
" is not for want of honeft attention to the fub-
" ject, that the end of the public miniftry of Je-
" fus was to reform the morals of men; and that
" THE PRINCIPAL USE OF MIRACLES WAS TO
" AWAKEN THEIR ATTENTION TO HIS PREACH-
" ING. When this was done, and chriftianity
" had got footing in the world, miracles became
" no longer neceffary. For as to any *new* doc-
" trines faid to be taught by chriftianity; or any

G 3

" new

" new method of falvation propofed; or any dif-
" coveries made which require fupernatural con-
" firmation; it is incumbent on thofe who main-
" tain their exiftence, to fhew what they are.
" For my own part, I freely confefs that I know of
" no fuch.   Had the preaching of Jefus contain-
" ed any thing of this kind, and had miracles
" been intended to give credibility to *what could*
" *not otherwife be proved*, then it fhould feem that
" miracles would be juft as neceffary to be per-
" formed *now*, as in the firft century: fince, as
" has been before obferved, it is not eafy to con-
" ceive how the *mere report* of a miraculous fact,
" which though probably true, yet may poffibly
" be falfe, can be admitted as fufficient evidence
" of a new doctrine, which is either incredible
" in itfelf, or unfupported by other evidence.

" But nothing furely could be farther from the
" intention of Jefus, than the introduction of a
" *new religion.*   He well knew this was impof-
" fible.   Religion, which is founded in the per-
" fections of God, and the nature of man, muft
" be

" be one invariable thing. Accordingly the doc-
" trines which he taught were precifely the fame
" with thofe of natural religion; which, if men
" could once be brought ferioufly to attend to
" them, wanted no other confirmation than that
" natural evidence, which St. Paul affirms to be
" fo full and complete as to leave thofe without
" excufe who neglect them, and to afford the
" moft entire fatisfaction to the fincere and im-
" partial mind. And as they wanted no addi-
" tional evidence, neither were they capable of
" any. What can the *hiftory of a miracle*, which
" muft always have fomething of uncertainty
" about it, do towards confirming a truth, which
" is already fupported by more than fufficient
" evidence of an indifputable kind ? If I would
" difcourfe for inftance on the Being and Provi-
" dence of GOD, it may, perhaps, be neceffary to
" work a miracle in order to fecure an audience;
" but is it poffible to conceive, that any *hiftory* of
" a miracle which I fhall be able to relate, can
" add any thing to that irrefiftible torrent of evi-

" dence

" dence on thefe great fubjects, which pours in
" from every furrounding object * ?

" The fame obfervation may be extended
" to moral truths, and to a future ftate. The
" *natural revelation* which it has pleafed GOD to
" give of thefe important truths is, in moft cafes,
" clear and certain : and if it be not always equal
" to mathematical demonftration, it is ftill abun-
" dantly fufficient to furnifh very powerful mo-
" tives for the regulation of the conduct; which
" is all that can be hoped for from the proudeft
" claim to fupernatural communication: with
" this unfpeakable advantage in favour of na-

* Quid poteft effe tam apertum, tamque perfpicuum, cum
coelum fufpeximus, cœleftiaque contemplati fumus, quam
effe aliquod numen præftantiffimæ mentis, quo hæc regan-
tur ?

When we lift our eyes to the heavens, and contemplate
the celeftial bodies, what can be more clearly evident, than
the exiftence of fome fuperior being of confummate wifdom,
by whom they are governed ?

Cic. de Natur. Deor. Lib. ii. Cap. 2.

The heavens declare the glory of GOD, and the firmament
fheweth his handy work. Day unto day uttereth fpeech, and
night unto night fheweth knowledge. There is no fpeech
nor language where their voice is not heard.—Pfalm xix.

" tural

" tural religion, that whoever undertakes to in-
" culcate its pure and falutary maxims, is on a
" footing of perfect equality with his fellow men.
" He can affume no dictatorial authority, nor ex-
" act from them any implicit obedience. As he
" cannot have the fhadow of pretence for ' do-
" minion over their faith,' he muft content him-
" felf with being the ' helper of their joy*.'

" To this natural evidence however, be it more
" or lefs, it is certain that our great inftructor ap-
" pealed. He pointed to the lilies of the field,
" and to the birds of the air; and taught men
" to deduce the doctrine of an eternal Provi-
" dence from the provifion made for fparrows.
" He argued from the paternal character, the
" readinefs of the one GOD and father of all, to
" hear the prayers of his intelligent and moral
" offspring, and to beftow upon the rightly dif-
" pofed mind, with no fparing hand, whatever
" can promote its real welfare. He adverted to
" the dignity of the human nature, fo noble in
" reafon! fo infinite in faculties! and of fo

* 2 Cor. i. 24.

" much

" much higher deſtination than the merely ve-
" getable and animal creation; and he exhort-
" ed his hearers, in the moſt perſuaſive language,
" not to waſte their lives in an unremitting at-
" tention to the periſhing objects of time and
" ſenſe, as if immortal minds were of no more
" value than the ' graſs which to-day is in the
" field, and to-morrow is caſt into the oven *,'
" but to ' provide themſelves a treaſure in the
" heavens that ſaileth not, where no thief ap-
" proacheth, neither moth corrupteth ✝!' But
" before our divine teacher could have any op-
" portunity of thus inſtructing the multitude, be-
" fore he could bring them to liſten to his inva-
" luable teaching, it was neceſſary to awaken their
" drowſy minds by the ſplendour of his miracles.

" This I imagine to have been the great
" end of miracles, ſuppoſing them to have been
" really performed; of which I have already ac-
" knowledged we can have no *certainty*. I can-
" not, however, help thinking it probable, be-
" cauſe it appears that in a very ſurpriſing de-

* Luke xii. 28.　　　† Luke xii. 33.

" gree

" gree this great end was happily effected. The
" being, the perfections, the moral providence of
" GOD, and the future expectations of man, be-
" came a favourite ftudy; and men of all ranks
" and degrees, as well the fcientific as the illi-
" terate, became defirous of knowing more per-
" fectly, that ' love of GOD which paffeth know-
" ledge !' The confequences of this turn given
" to the tafte of mankind, if the expreffion may
" be allowed, were in the higheft degree favour-
" able to morals. The conduct of thofe who
" joined themfelves to the chriftian name, though
" not in all inftances alike, was yet generally fo
" pure and peaceable, their tempers fo kind and
" benevolent, their patience under fufferings fo
" eminent, and their hope of immortality fo
" triumphant, that the followers of Jefus became
" the admiration of the world; and ' the joy that
" was fet before him,' and for which he fo cheer-
" fully fubmitted to the malice of the enemies of
" truth and virtue, feemed now to be no longer
" in profpect, but to be actually realized.

My

My friend, warmed by his fubject, ftill pro-. ceeded.

" What a delightful ftate of things," faid he, " could this primitive fimplicity have been pre- " ferved! But, alas! how foon was the glory of " this great reformation obfcured. The pride " of the heathen converts, in imitation of that " abfurd fuperftition from which they had been " fo lately called, began to exalt its humble foun- " der into a God, a title which, when on earth, " he would have rejected with abhorrence. " When they had proceeded thus far, they fan- " cied that the doctrines which he taught, fo " confonant to the uncorrupted fentiments of the " human mind, were too plain and fimple to " be worthy of fo great a being. They would " have chriftianity to be fomething myfterious " and incomprehenfible; fomething to aftonifh " and confound the underftanding, inftead of en- " lighting and inftructing it; and, O fatal and " deplorable error! fomething by means of which " an *eftablifhed and endowed priefthood* might be
" enabled

" enabled to maintain and increafe its power and
" authority over the people. To this end, while
" they made light of the truths of natural reli-
." gion, the eternal rock on which pure chrifti-
" anity was founded, they invented and propa-
" gated, with furious zeal, the fictions of original
" fin, election and reprobation, eternal punifh-
" ment, fatisfaction for fin by the death of Chrift,
" church authority, and a number of facraments
" to be adminiftered by facred hands—all irre-
" concileable with right reafon, and the perfec-
" tions of Deity, but all wonderfully calculated
" to keep in awe the ignorant, who are always
" the great majority of mankind *. The light
" which

---

* Ignorance and credulity have ever been companions, and
have mifled and enflaved mankind; philofophy has in all ages
endeavoured to oppofe their progrefs, and to loofen the
fhackles they had impofed. Philofophers have on this account been called unbelievers. Unbelievers of what? of the
fictions of fancy, of witchcraft, hobgoblins, apparitions, vam-
pires, fairies; of the influence of ftars on human actions, miracles wrought by the bones of faints, the flight of ominous
birds, the predictions of the bowels of dying animals, expound-
ers of dreams, fortunetellers, conjurers, modern prophets, ne-
cromancy, chiromancy, animal magnetifm, with endlefs variety

" which Jefus and his difciples had thrown on
" moral fubjeds became almoft extinguifhed;
" and the fhort triumph of knowledge and virtue,
" was fucceeded by a long and difmal night of ig-
" norance, fuperftition, and tyranny, from which
" we are at this day only beginning to emerge.

" A beginning however has certainly been
" made. The labours of learned and fincere
" enquirers after truth, have demonftrated that
" many things heretofore fuppofed effential to
" chriftianity, neither belong to *it*, nor to *any*
" true fyftem of religion. As free inveftigation

---

riety of folly? Thefe they have difbelieved and defpifed, but
have ever bowed their hoary heads to Truth and Nature.

Mankind may be divided in refpect to the facility of their
belief or conviction, into two claffes; thofe who are ready to
affent to fingle facts from the evidence of their fenfes, or
from the ferious affertions of others; and thofe who require
analogy to corroborate or authenticate them.———This analogy pre-fuppofes an acquired knowledge of things; hence
children and ignorant people are the moft credulous, as not
poffeffing much knowledge of the ufual courfe of nature; and
fecondly, thofe are moft credulous whofe faculty of comparing
ideas, or the voluntary exertion of it, is flow and imperfect. Of
this kind are the bulk of mankind; they continue throughout
their lives in a ftate of childhood, and have thus been *the dupes
of priefts and politicians in all ages and in all countries of the
world.*   DARWIN'S Zoonomia.

" proceeds,

" proceeds, the load of abfurdity under which
" truth has fo long been buried, will by degrees
" be removed, and it will be reftored to its na-
" tive beauty. Amongft other particulars, I have
" no hefitation in fuppofing, that it already ap-
" pears with fufficient evidence, that Jefus, about
" whofe perfon and office the world has fo long
" and fo widely differed, was no other than what
" his immediate followers defcribed him to have
" been in their firft public difcourfes after his
" death, namely, ' A MAN, APPROVED OF GOD,
" BY MIRACLES AND WONDERS AND SIGNS
" WHICH GOD DID BY HIM;' that is, an emi-
" nent teacher of moral and religious truth,
" whofe labours it pleafed heaven in an extraor-
" dinary manner to affift; but who had no other
" doctrine to inculcate, becaufe there was no
" other which it concerned mankind to know,
" than thofe which, however fadly neglected, had
" been always known, namely, an univerfal Pro-
" vidence, a future ftate, and the abfolute necef-
" fity of applying before all things to the cultiva-
" tion of the moral powers, in order to anfwer

3   " the

" the true end, and to attain to the higheſt en-
" joyment of our being.

" If in this attempt to delineate chriſtianity,"
continued my friend, " I have been ſuccefsful, it
" will appear to be entitled to regard, not on the
" footing of *authority*, but on account of its in-
" trinſic excellence, the importance of its doc-
" trines, the purity of its moral, and the foli-
" dity of its reaſonings ; and the queſtion con-
" cerning the reality of miracles, may be diſcuſſ-
" ed with the utmoſt calmneſs and impartiality,
" and even with *perfect indifference as to the reſult.*

" For if, after fair enquiry, they ſhould appear to
" any man to be the invention of early chriſtians,
" warmly but indiſcreetly zealous for the honour
" of their illuſtrious teacher, ſuch an one will have
" the ſatisfaction to reflect, that all that is valu-
" able in the New Teſtament, all that entitles it
" to ſuperior eſtimation in compariſon with other
" books, will remain unaffected by this diſcovery.
" While, on the other hand, thoſe who, after the
" ſame diſpaſſionate enquiry, ſhall be of opinion,
" that the reality of miracles is ſupported by the
                                          " higheſt

" higheſt probability, which is the utmoſt that
" can be rationally aſſerted, will ſtill conſider
" them, not as proofs of the truth of chriſtianity
" to this diſtant age, but as expedients to gain
" attention to it from thoſe to whom it was ori-
" ginally addreſſed. In our ſituation, *it is not the*
" *miracles that prove the truth of the religion; but*
" *it is the truth of the religion that proves the mi-*
" *ricles.* It is the PERFECTION OF THE DOC-
" TRINE which is itſelf the *grand miracle,* and
" which renders probable all the reſt. Imagine
" for a moment the abſence of this eſſential cir-
" cumſtance, and all the learning of a Lardner *
                                            " will

---

* With the writings of this great man I had but a very
ſlight acquaintance till in 1788, Mr. Johnſon, much to his
honour, favoured the world with a complete and accurate edi-
tion in eleven volumes 8vo. at a very low price. I then began
ſeriouſly to ſtudy the vaſt maſs of evidence which tho learned
and laborious author had collected, to prove the genuineneſs of
the books of the New Teſtament, and the authenticity of the
Goſpel hiſtory, upon the ground of teſtimony. But what was
the effect upon my mind? Nothing ſhort of an entire conviction of the extreme obſcurity and difficulty in which the
ſubject is involved. Upon enquiry amongſt the intelligent
part of my acquaintance, I found to my ſurpriſe that my caſe
was by no means ſingular. And I am ſtrongly inclined to be-

" will be infufficient to fhew, that the wonders
" of the New Teftament are entitled to any
" higher credit, than the fables of Æfop, or the
" fictions of Homer."

Here, though I was far from wifhing it, it became neceffary to put an end to the converfation. I took leave of my friend with thanks for
his unreferved communication, and fully determined to reconfider the fubject; and I hope my
reader is in the fame difpofition.

lieve, that the general effect of reading this elaborate work
will be very different indeed from that which the excellent
author intended.

THE END.

Printed by Thomas Benfley, Bolt-Court, Fleet-Street, London.